DATE DUE

THE CHICAGO FIRE

Look for these and other exciting
World Disasters books:

THE CHICAGO FIRE

by
Lois Warburton

Illustrations by Maurie Manning

and
Michael Spackman
Robert Caldwell
Randol Eagles

LUCENT
B·O·O·K·S

WORLD DISASTERS

Library of Congress Cataloging-in-Publication Data

Warburton, Lois, 1938-
    Chicago fire / by Lois Warburton; illustrations by Maurie Manning.
      p.   cm. -- (World disasters)
    Bibliography: p.
    Includes index.
    Summary: An account of the fire that raged for twenty-four hours over much of Chicago in October 1871, destroying property and homes and killing at least 300 people.
    ISBN 1-56006-002-6
    1. Fires--Illinois--Chicago--History--19th century--Juvenile literature. 2. Chicago (Ill.)--History--To 1875--Juvenile literature. [1. Fires--Illinois--Chicago--History--19th century. 2. Chicago (Ill.)--History--To 1875.] I. Manning, Maurie 1960- ill. II. Title III. Series.
F548.42.W15 1989
977.3'11041--dc20

          89-33554
          CIP
          AC

*To my parents,
my best and favorite teachers*

Table of Contents

Preface
The World Disasters Series

World disasters have always aroused human curiosity. Whenever news of tragedy spreads, we want to learn more about it. We wonder how and why the disaster happened, how people reacted, and whether we might have acted differently. To be sure, disaster evokes a wide range of responses—fear, sorrow, despair, generosity, even hope. Yet from every great disaster, one remarkable truth always seems to emerge: in spite of death, pain, and destruction, the human spirit triumphs.

History is full of great disasters, which arise from a variety of causes. Earthquakes, floods, volcanic eruptions, and other natural events often produce widespread destruction. Just as often, however, people accidentally bring suffering and distress on themselves and other human beings. And many disasters have sinister causes, like human greed, envy, or prejudice.

The disasters included in this series have been chosen not only for their dramatic qualities, but also for their educational value. The reader will learn about the causes and effects of the greatest disasters in history. Technical concepts and interesting anecdotes are explained and illustrated in inset boxes.

But disasters should not be viewed in isolation. To enrich the reader's understanding, these books present historical information about the time period, and interesting facts about the culture in which each disaster occurred. Finally, they teach valuable lessons about human nature. More acts of bravery, cowardice, intelligence, and foolishness are compressed into the few days of a disaster than most people experience in a lifetime.

Dramatic illustrations and evocative narrative lure the reader to distant cities and times gone by. Readers witness the awesome power of an exploding volcano, the magnitude of a violent earthquake, and the hopelessness of passengers on a mighty ship passing to its watery grave. By reliving the events, the reader will see how disaster affects the lives of real people and will gain a deeper understanding of their sorrow, their pain, their courage, and their hope.

Introduction
Fire and Wind

On the night of Sunday, October 8, 1871, a strong wind blew through the streets of Chicago, blowing dust into every crack. Downtown, fire watchman Mathias Schaffer paced the rooftop of the Cook County Courthouse scanning the dry city for any sign of flames. It had been an unusually hot and dry year. There had been twenty-seven fires in the city just the week before, so he was not surprised when he spotted flames across the river on the city's West Side. Quickly he called down to William Brown, the fire-alarm operator in the Courthouse, to sound the alarm at the fire station nearest the flames.

But Schaffer made a mistake. He chose the wrong station and the alarm sounded in a station located almost a mile (1.61 kilometers) from the fire. By the time the first fire engines arrived, the fire had destroyed the barn belonging to Catherine and Patrick O'Leary and five other houses and barns were in flames. The fire spread rapidly, whipped by 60-mile-per-hour winds (96.6-kilometer-per-hour). Before the firemen realized it, the fire was out of control. It consumed the buildings in the O'Leary's block and spread rapidly north through the West Side. It was not long before the fierce winds blew a shower of sparks and burning debris into the air and carried them across the river where they landed on rooftops on the South Side, igniting downtown Chicago.

It was the beginning of the Great Chicago Fire, the worst fire in Chicago's history and one of the most famous disasters in American history. According to legend, the fire began when Mrs. O'Leary's cow kicked over a lantern. No one knows for certain how it started. But when the flames died down 26 hours later, they had devastated 3.5 miles (5.65 kilometers) of the city, including most of downtown Chicago, destroyed 17,450 buildings, left almost 100,000 people homeless, and claimed about 250 lives.

Today, the event is still known in Chicago simply as the Great Fire. It was such a setback for this growing and prosperous city that today people still fondly refer to the period of Chicago's history before that October day in 1871 as simply, "before the fire." This was a time of great promise for a city that was fast becoming a major commercial center of North America.

The Chicago Fire's Place in History

————Declaration of Independence signed — 1776

——————————————— **1800** ————————————————
——— **Chicago's first settlers establish Fort Dearborn — 1804**

——— Illinois statehood — 1818
——— Erie Canal completed — 1824
——— First commercial railroad line in the U.S. — 1827

——— First railroad line through Chicago — 1848

——— Raising of Chicago begins — 1856
——— Abraham Lincoln president of the U.S. — 1861-1865
——— American Civil War — 1861-1865
——— Golden spike completes the transcontinental railroad — 1869
——— **Chicago Fire — 1871**
——— International Association of Fire Chiefs established — 1873

——— First entirely steel-framed building erected in Chicago — 1890

——————————————— **1900** ————————————————
——— Fire in Chicago's Iroquois Theater kills 575 people — 1903
——— San Francisco Fire kills 500 people — 1906
——— Factory fire in New York City kills 146 people — 1911
——— World War I — 1914-1918

——— Chicago World's Fair — 1933

——— Fire in Boston's Cocoanut Grove nightclub kills 491 people — 1942
——— World War II — 1939-1945

——— School in Chicago burns, killing 95 people — 1958
——— John F. Kennedy assassinated — 1963

——— Neil Armstrong walks on the moon — 1969

——— MGM Grand Hotel in Las Vegas burns, killing 85 people — 1980

One

Queen City of the West

A steam engine pulling a line of train cars puffed smoke from its stack as it clattered alongside the Chicago River. In 1871, Chicago was the crossroads between the established eastern states and the new, growing territories of the West. Every day trains to and from Milwaukee, Detroit, St. Louis, Des Moines, and Minneapolis passed through Chicago.

Steamships from the East, which had already sailed up the Erie Canal, then through the Great Lakes to Lake Michigan, entered Chicago by way of the Chicago River. The river banks were dotted with tall **grain elevators** full of grain to be shipped east. Behind them, smoke poured from the chimney stacks of factories where farm equipment and furniture were produced. Huge stacks of lumber were piled up at lumber mills along the river. The odor of sewage and the stench from Chicago's stockyards hung in the air.

Beyond the factories and grain elevators were streets full of stores. The store windows displayed everything from dresses and jewelry to cooking pots and wood-burning stoves. Wooden sidewalks were bustling with people busy shopping and delivering goods. In the distance, church spires soared above the wooden rooftops.

Although Chicago was a young city, its fast growth and prosperity had already earned it the title Queen of the West. The wide fork of the Chicago River formed a rough T-shape, and the branches divided the city into three parts: the North Side, South Side, and West Side. The North Side was primarily an upper-class residential area. The South Side contained Chicago's bustling business district, as well as both the wealthiest and poorest neighborhoods in the city. The West Side was almost entirely covered by the small, wood-frame houses and shacks of Chicago's working class.

The three sections of the city were connected by twelve drawbridges. Each bridge had a bridge tender. He operated the drawbridge from his seat near the center of the bridge. Every time a ship approached, the bridge tender turned the bridge ninety degrees on its center pivot so it swung out over the water. The ship could then pass between the bridge and the shore. Each time the bridge was opened, lines of wagons and pedestrians backed up on the banks, waiting for the tender to turn the bridge back so they could cross the river.

In 1871, Chicago's population was nearly 330,000. It had grown from 30,000 in just twenty years! The growth really began in the 1830s when pioneers from the East were heading west on covered wagons. Later they came by train and steamship.

The city was also flooded with waves of **immigrants** from Europe. They came to Chicago looking for opportunity. They wanted to provide their families with better homes, better educations, and a better future than most of them could have hoped for in Europe.

They soon discovered that Chicago's streets were not paved with gold. Few obtained the riches they had dreamed of, but with hard work, most of them were able to earn a decent living. The immigrants provided the labor that built Chicago. They dug canals, slaughtered hogs, laid railroad lines, built farm equipment, sewed dresses, milled lumber, and served the rich, all for very low wages. Though most immigrants remained poor, many saved enough to buy their own small, wooden homes in crowded neighborhoods on Chicago's West Side.

Together, immigrants and American pioneers created a population explosion in Chicago. And, since all those people needed homes, food, clothing, and services of all kinds, a great building boom soon followed.

Chicago's building boom began in the 1830s. The streets were full of **land speculators** making fortunes by buying land cheap and then selling it for a profit. Even shop owners ran out of their stores to stop people on the sidewalk with offers of houses, farms, and desirable corner lots for sale. A lot that sold for one hundred dollars in 1832 was worth three thousand in 1834 and an amazing fifteen thousand dollars in 1835. Real estate speculation was like a fever, and almost everyone caught it.

When the building boom got under way, Chicago was transformed into a dynamic, chaotic, muddy city. Temporary, wooden buildings appeared overnight. No matter how many homes, hotels, stores, saloons, churches, schools, and meeting halls were built, more were soon needed.

Not every building in the city was made of wood. Mansions, churches, and public buildings were constructed of bricks and limestone, often reinforced with iron. Their owners boasted that they were fireproof. But buildings of brick and stone were too expensive for most people.

It had not been easy for the city to

WHERE IS CHICAGO?

Chicago, Illinois, is located on the southwest corner of Lake Michigan at the mouth of the Chicago River. Since its early days, it has been an important transportation crossroads. Except for crossing the land between the Chicago and Illinois rivers, a boat could travel all the way from the Atlantic Ocean, through the Great Lakes, and down the Mississippi River to the Gulf of Mexico.

This meant that whoever controlled the land route, or **portage**, between the Chicago and Illinois rivers controlled all transporation through the area. The city of Chicago actually began in 1804 as Fort Dearborn, an army fort built to protect this key portage.

keep up with the sudden growth. Its dirt streets were dusty in the summer and muddy the rest of the year. The water supply was inadequate and far from pure. From time to time, someone catching water from the faucet also caught a small fish. And with one wooden building after another going up, fire was a constant threat.

The streets, however, were the citizens' priority. By 1856, the mud and potholes were so bad that they had become the source of many jokes. Signs saying "TEAM UNDERNEATH" and "STAGE DROPPED THROUGH" were posted at particularly bad spots. Someone once left a hat beside a sign declaring "MAN LOST." Wooden planks were laid on some streets as a substitute for paving, but when heavy carriages ran over them, mud squirted between the planks onto surprised pedestrians.

In 1856, city officials chose an astounding solution to their problem. They decided to raise the entire city above the mud and resurface Chicago's marshy bottom with earth and stone. Between 1856 and 1876, all the buildings within the city limits were raised

4 to 10 feet (1.25 to 3 meters). Using hand-operated **jackscrews**, a crew of men could lift a small house and leave it sitting on the jacks while they filled in underneath with earth and stone. Sometimes every building in a block was moved to a new location and replaced by stone buildings. Every day during this period, one saw the bizarre scene of houses rolling down the streets and five-story buildings perched on stilts.

The "raising" of Chicago left some rather odd features. The space underneath some of the raised buildings was not filled in with earth and stone. That created a maze of underground passageways and caverns under parts of the city. And, because some owners were slow to raise their buildings, the new, wooden sidewalks, which were also raised on stilts, rose and fell like roller coasters to reach every doorstep.

Supplying Chicago's growing population with enough safe drinking water presented the city with another serious challenge. Lake Michigan contained all the water Chicago needed, but the waterworks system could not deliver it fast enough. Also, the lake water near the shore was polluted. Factories, slaughterhouses, and sewers dumped waste directly into the Chicago River, and the river flowed into the lake, taking the waste with it.

To reach clean water, a tunnel was built 2 miles (3.25 kilometers) out into the lake. At the end of the tunnel was a water intake called a **crib**, a huge box that screened the water entering the tunnel. The crib rose above the lake's surface and was topped by a small house where the crib tender lived. In 1871, John Tolland was Chicago's crib tender.

Chicago's new water system was an extraordinary engineering feat for the time. Besides the tunnel and crib, it included a 130-foot (39 meter) water tower and a pumping station by the lakeshore. This station pumped water through 154 miles (248 kilometers) of pipes in the city. Completed in 1869, the new system was the pride of Chicago.

Besides providing drinking water, the new water system was intended to help solve another serious problem: fire. In fact, insurance agents in Chicago called the West Side 'The Red Flash' because it was so prone to fire.

Actually, the entire city deserved that name. In 1870 alone, Chicago had more than six hundred fires. One reason there were so many fires was the common use of wood in building homes, sidewalks, fences, and streets. Even stone buildings had wooden floors, roofs, and decorations.

Chicago was also full of wooden warehouses packed with **flammable** goods. The river was lined with wooden ships and crossed by wooden drawbridges. There were lumber mills with piles of sawdust, grain elevators five stories high full of flammable grain, and factories with piles of coal needed to run the steam engines. There were also thousands of homes with stacks of fire-

HOW TO RAISE A FIVE-STORY BUILDING

At five stories high the Tremont House was the largest hotel in Chicago. In 1861, when engineer George Pullman was hired to raise the Tremont, everyone thought he was attempting an impossible task. But Pullman was sure he could do it. He gathered together five thousand **jackscrews** and hired a crew of twelve hundred men. Then, over a period of many days, he very slowly and carefully raised the hotel eight feet. The hotel's guests knew what was happening only because the front steps got steeper every day. They lived in the hotel the entire time.

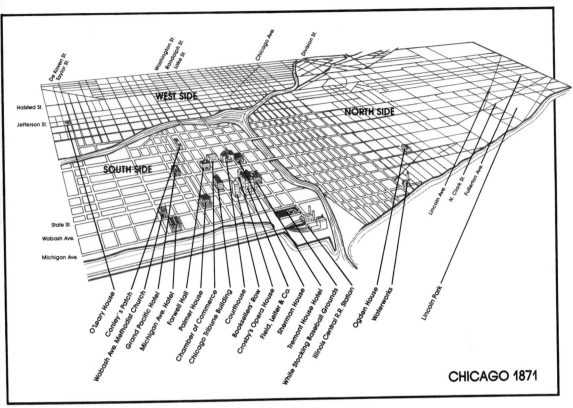

CHICAGO 1871

wood and barrels of lamp oil, and, perhaps most hazardous of all, barns full of **combustible** hay.

The city had tried hard to equip and prepare its fire department. It owned seventeen steam-driven fire engines, or **steamers**. Besides the steamers, Chicago had twenty-three hose carts, four hook and ladder wagons, and two **hose elevators**. These elevators had platforms that lifted firefighters almost two stories high so they could aim water onto roofs and upper stories.

The new telegraphic alarm system, installed during the 1860s, was another important addition to fire fighting. Alarms, sent from new, easy-to-operate alarm boxes throughout the city, went directly to the central office in the courthouse. From there, signals, numbered according to the location of the boxes, were sent to the fire stations. The alarm boxes were locked to prevent false alarms, and trustworthy citizens who lived nearby kept the keys.

To back up the alarm system, watchmen were posted as lookouts on the roof of the courthouse, and the courthouse bell tolled out the alarm number. In addition, between 9:30 P.M. and 6:00 A.M., watchmen were assigned to the roof of each fire station.

Of course, all this equipment and preparation would have been worthless without a reliable supply of water for fighting fires. Technically at least, the new waterworks, with its pumping station and tall water tower, put all the water in Lake Michigan at the city's disposal.

Two
City Life

By 1871, Chicago had become the railroad, meat-packing, lumber, and grain center of America. In many ways, it was gradually becoming a cleaner, healthier, more livable city. Shoppers and businessmen thronged to new stores and businesses along State Street. Local children attended a highly rated public school system. Visitors stayed in luxurious hotels and strolled the new, green parks that ringed the city.

By far the most exciting part of Chicago was the downtown section on the South Side. This is where most of the public buildings were located, as well as the largest department stores, hotels, and businesses.

One of the landmarks of the downtown area was the Tribune Building on the corner of Dearborn and Madison Streets. The home of Chicago's largest newspaper, this expensive, four-story stone structure was supposed to be "absolutely fireproof." Joe Medill, co-publisher of the *Chicago Tribune*, had noticed, however, that the "fireproof" material covering the roof seemed to get soft on hot, sunny days.

One block north of the Tribune Building was Crosby's Opera House on Washington Street. This entertainment hall had been closed all summer for extensive renovations, and the grand re-opening was scheduled for Monday, October 9.

Another landmark was the courthouse, which occupied the block at Clark and Randolph Streets in the center of the city.

The middle portion of the courthouse had been built of wood in 1853, and in 1858, a huge, stone wing had been added to either side of the wooden structure. The west wing contained Chicago's city hall and the new fire-alarm dispatch center. The east wing held the Cook County Courthouse and jail. The center portion was topped by a two-story tower that had a bell inside and a walkway around the outside. Every night a watchman patrolled that walkway to watch for fire.

One of the most fashionable streets in downtown Chicago was State Street. The gracious stone buildings that lined this newly paved street contained some of the most fashionable shops and suc-

cessful businesses in town. Many of Chicago's richest and most powerful citizens could be found walking along its new, wooden sidewalks, popping in and out of the First National Bank, the St. James Hotel, or Field, Leiter & Co.'s department store.

The scene was a little quieter on Michigan Avenue, two blocks east of State Street. With the lake on one side of the tree-lined street and rows of elegant three-story mansions on the other, this broad avenue was a serene haven for many of the wealthiest people in Chicago. There, the private Chicago Club was always a good place to find some of the city's leading citizens relaxing and conversing.

18

Just a short walk from Michigan Avenue was an entirely different side of Chicago. Its booming business and rapid growth were also alluring to criminals. Fifth Avenue was the heart of Chicago's worst slum—a three-block area called Conley's Patch. This run-down neighborhood of pawnshops, saloons, brothels, and dilapidated cottages and boardinghouses was only three blocks from the courthouse and four blocks from the luxurious shops of State Street.

Conley's Patch was the vice district of Chicago in 1871, and while all the honest citizens of Chicago were eagerly going about their business, the criminals who lived there were going about theirs just as eagerly.

The increasing prosperity of the city created many opportunities for thieves. As a commercial and transportation center, the city was always full of newcomers and transients. They were easy prey for con men and pickpockets. And Chicago's wide-open frontier spirit made it quite easy to tempt local politicians and police officers with bribes. Because of this, the illegal activities that occurred at Conley's Patch were tolerated by city officials, including the police, who seldom bothered its unruly inhabitants. Also because of this, many of Chicago's criminals were colorful characters, daring and open about their activities.

One of the city's most colorful criminals was the petite Roger Plant, an immigrant from England who stood just over 5 feet tall (1.5 meters) in boots. Despite his size, Roger controlled a vast criminal empire. He ran his profitable network of gambling rooms and brothels from his headquarters in a run-down building in Conley's Patch known as

THE TENANTS OF ROGER'S BARRACKS

The ramshackle, underground rooms maintained by Roger Plant were home to many criminals. Among them was the infamous safecracker Speckled Jimmy Calwell, who was the first burglar known to use tape to bind and gag his victims. Calwell is also credited with being the first person to use a bomb threat to extort money from a company.

Mary Brennan ran a pickpocket school for young girls. Her "students" had to pick a minimum of five pockets a day, plus snatch purses and shoplift. The underground tenants at Roger's Barracks were so infamous that a new term arose for them: the **underworld.**

Roger's Barracks. By the time Plant had finished adding rooms onto this unkempt, wooden structure, it covered over half a block. Most of it was full of rooms used for drinking, gambling, prostitution, and other vices.

By far the most notorious part of Roger's Barracks was the maze of tunnels and caves underneath it. These were the old building foundations, left unfilled when the city was raised for drainage purposes in the 1850s and 1860s. The sixty underground rooms were filled with criminals and misfits of all types, who paid Plant over-priced rents to keep the police away.

THE CHICAGO WHITE STOCKINGS

Chicago's first professional baseball team, the White Stockings, was organized in 1870. The White Stockings baseball field was located near the Great Central Train Depot in downtown Chicago. Since players did not have contracts, the White Stockings stole the best players from Eastern teams by paying them as much as $2,500 a season. In those days, that was twice the normal salary. The result was an outstanding team that, in 1870, set the all-time record for the highest score in a professional baseball game by beating the Bluff Club from Memphis, Tennessee, 157-1. The White Stockings became the Chicago Cubs in 1902 when a new team became known as the Chicago White Sox.

To get away from the crowded South Side, more and more Chicagoans began moving out to the North Side — Chicago's first suburb. Just across the river from the South Side, the North Side was still only a short walk from downtown. It was primarily residential. Homes there ranged from the grand mansions of the wealthy to the small cottages of the middle class. The few factories, lumberyards, and other industries in this section of the city were located right along the river where they did not disturb the residents' peace and quiet. The pride of the North Side was the new waterworks tower on Chicago Avenue at the lakeshore. Mahlon Ogden and Chicago's other civic leaders considered it a symbol of the city's strength and ingenuity.

The luxurious home and grounds of Mr. and Mrs. Mahlon Ogden occupied an

entire block on Lafayette Place on the North Side. Ogden, whose brother had been the first mayor of Chicago, owned an insurance office downtown.

During the week, the Ogden's days were busy. Mr. Ogden went to work at his office on Lake Street in the South Side and attended many civic meetings. Meanwhile, Mrs. Ogden would see that their six servants had their orders for the day. She might spend part of her day meeting with a church committee.

Several afternoons a week, Mrs. Ogden held calling hours in her home. Friends and social climbers, all in their finest clothes, came to join her in her parlor for a few hours of stimulating conversation. Sometimes they played cards or a lively parlor game like charades. Or

perhaps someone might play the piano so they could have a sing-along.

The Ogden's evenings and weekends were just as busy. Wealthy people in the nineteenth century had a variety of activities to fill their leisure hours. They gave grand dinner parties with seven-course meals. They collected extravagant art objects and spent hours reading and discussing books.

They attended concerts and plays and joined their friends at lecture halls. Chicago was rapidly becoming a cultural center of national importance. The same opera and dramatic companies that performed on Broadway in New York City often came to Chicago to stage their productions at the Crosby Opera House and other theaters. And people from throughout Illinois and surrounding regions traveled to Chicago to see them.

Recreation for Chicago's working classes, people like Patrick and Catherine O'Leary, was provided by the city parks and the beach at the lake. Families and couples strolled, picnicked, rowed boats, swam, and played games. On broad park lawns, adults played croquet or pitched horseshoes, while their children played tag, rolled hoops, and ran races. For a picnic in the country, the city's residents could ride the cheap public **horsecars** out to the suburbs.

The O'Learys may have enjoyed taking their five children to the park to get away from their ramshackle, two-room cottage at 137 De Koven Street on the West Side.

The hard-working O'Learys were poor Irish immigrants. They lived in a crowded neighborhood that was a mixture of dirty, unpaved streets, unpainted, unmended fences, cluttered yards, and small, wooden houses. These were Chicago's lower-class neighborhoods, where more than 200,000 of the city's 330,000 residents lived.

Rows of similar neighborhoods, extending inland for several blocks, lined the branches of the Chicago River, especially the South Branch. The dilapidated, pine houses stood in the shadow of the city's main industries. Noise from the factories was constant. The air was rank with the smell from distilleries, meat-packing houses, and tanneries, and the river was polluted from their refuse. Crowded conditions, filth, and poverty brought widespread disease and death to people of all ages in these neighborhoods.

Patrick O'Leary was a poorly paid laborer, but by 1864, he and Catherine had saved enough to buy their own home for five hundred dollars. They managed to do this only because they had two additional sources of income. Catherine had a milk route in the neighborhood, and they had two cottages on their property. They rented one to another Irish family. They lived in the other. Behind the O'Learys' cottage was the small, wooden barn where Cather-

ine kept her horse, five cows, and a calf.

The O'Learys and their children often rose before dawn so they could complete their chores before breakfast. After breakfast, on workdays, Patrick took his lunch pail full of bread and cold potatoes and walked to his job where he would work until dark. The three oldest children, with lunch pails in hand, walked to school. Catherine had to milk her cows and deliver milk to her customers before she could eat. Then she would spend her day taking care of four-year-old Mary and the baby, James. She did this while tending the cows, cleaning the house and barn, shopping, sewing and mending clothing, baking and cooking, chopping firewood, and making butter.

Sunday was the O'Learys' only day for leisure. Patrick and the children could sleep until it was time to go to church, but Catherine still got up at 5:00 A.M. to milk her cows. After church, the family was free to visit with friends and neighbors or go to the park.

Sunday, October 8, 1871, would have been a good day to spend in the park because it was unseasonably warm. There had been no rain for three weeks, very little since July, and the wind blew dust into every crack. But Catherine had a sore foot and wanted to rest. By early evening, her foot hurt badly, so she put three of her children to bed and was in bed herself before 8:00 P.M.

Patrick, who had to leave for work early in the morning, was preparing to go to bed at the same time, when Daniel Sullivan, who lived across the street, dropped in to visit. He found that Catherine had gone to bed, so after chatting with Patrick for a few minutes, he left. Daniel walked home, but before going inside, he sat down on the curb and listened awhile to the merriment at the McLaughlin's, who rented the O'Learys' second cottage. They were celebrating the arrival of Mrs. McLaughlin's brother from Ireland.

Three
The Great Fire

Shortly after 9:00 P.M., Daniel Sullivan suddenly saw a flame burst through the side of the O'Learys' barn. "Fire! Fire! Fire!" Sullivan yelled as he ran across the street to the barn. Although he had a peg leg, he dashed through the front door of the barn and untied two cows, which then refused to move. The heat was intense, and the flames leapt behind him. Having no time to untie the horse or the other cows, he hurried toward the back door. Suddenly he slipped on the wet, plank floor and fell down hard. Hampered by his peg leg, he struggled to his feet and limped his way to the door. He was almost there when a calf, wailing in pain and terror, ran into him. Its back was on fire. He grabbed its rope and pulled it out just as the barn dissolved in flames.

At that moment, other neighbors began to arrive. The O'Learys' house, only 40 feet (12 meters) away from the barn, was already **smoldering**, but all the O'Learys were still asleep. Dennis Rogan, a neighbor, ran into the house, yelling to wake the family. Catherine, in spite of her sore foot, rushed out to try to save her new wagon, but the fire was too hot. Patrick and a crowd of neighbors began pouring water on the house. Several times the house caught fire, but each time they put it out. Next door, the Daltons were not so fortunate. The wind whipped the flames across the narrow space between the O'Learys' barn and their house and quickly destroyed it. The Daltons were the first family left homeless by the Great Chicago Fire.

The fire did not catch Chicago completely unprepared. The city was justifiably proud of its modern, well-equipped fire department. With a new alarm system in place and a recently completed waterworks system to back it up, the

Chicago Fire Department thought it was ready for the worst. But its resources had been severely tested in the week preceding the Great Fire. On Sunday night when the Great Fire started, several firemen were still guarding the dying embers of a fire that had started the night before in a woodworking factory on the West Side. Many of the city's firefighters were exhausted, and much of their equipment needed repair.

Just the same, the fire department might have succeeded in controlling the blaze in the O'Learys' block if it had not been for a few costly errors. First, the two fire alarms reportedly sent from a drugstore in the O'Learys' neighborhood at 9:05 P.M. and 9:15 P.M. were never received. Then, at 9:30 P.M., when Mathias Schaffer, the fire watchman on the downtown courthouse roof, spotted the flames, he misjudged their location. Schaffer mistakenly ordered William Brown, the fire-alarm operator in the courthouse, to telegraph a signal to the fire stations indicating that a fire had broken out near alarm box 342, nearly a mile (1.6 kilometers) from the O'Learys' house. So the station nearest the O'Learys' did not respond first. And the fire engines first sent went to the wrong location losing valuable time searching for the fire.

When Schaffer realized his mistake, he told Brown to strike the correct alarm. Brown, for reasons never understood, refused and struck 342 again. Because of this, the *Williams*, the city's newest fire engine, which could throw 700 gallons (2,653 liters) of water a minute, did not respond in time. If it had, the *Williams* probably would have stopped the fire from spreading.

Meanwhile firemen in two fire stations on the West Side spotted the fire themselves and responded. They were the first firefighters on the scene, and by the time they arrived, six barns and houses were burning. They immediately began hosing water onto the fire, but it was already spreading rapidly. When the third engine reached De Koven Street, three buildings at the north end of the block were ablaze. Volunteers were organized to train water on that fire, but after a few minutes, they scattered, abandoning the hose and another opportunity to contain the fire. Shortly after Fire Marshall Robert Williams arrived on De Koven Street at 10:00 P.M., the fire leaped across the street and into the next block.

The exhausted firemen and their overworked equipment could not control the fire. Steam engines failed, hoses broke, and reinforcements were slow to arrive. The firefighters, who had to work close to the fire to make their equipment effective, were constantly driven back by its intense heat. And all this time, the wind grew stronger and stronger, fanning the fire, which lit up the night sky. Sparks, embers, and burning debris formed a red shower that blew high overhead and landed on dry roofs, steeples, and stacks of lumber.

The wind was so fierce, it blew a shower of sparks 3 miles east (4.8 kilometers), out over Lake Michigan. By 11:00 P.M., so many fiery sparks were landing on the crib tender's home that John Tolland was alarmed. The wind had churned the lake into giant waves, so escape by boat was impossible. Tolland sent his wife to bed, then gathered a broom and six buckets. All alone, for five

hours, under a barrage of sparks sometimes as thick as hail, he poured water over his home and swept sparks from the roof. Finally, by 4:00 A.M., most of the red storm had moved north. John Tolland had saved his home and family.

All this time, the fire spread rapidly toward the South Branch of the Chicago River. In the confusion, panic set in. Owners of shops and saloons fled for their lives, leaving their buildings open and unattended. Looters ran into the deserted shops and loaded their arms with merchandise.

SPONTANEOUS COMBUSTION

Sometimes a fire can start, or *ignite*, all by itself. This is called spontaneous **combustion**. It occurs when a material generates its own heat by chemical changes taking place in the material itself. If the heat has no way to escape, it will continue to rise until it reaches the ignition point of the material, which will burst into flames. That is why spontaneous combustion is a safety hazard in closed rooms or buildings with poor ventilation.

Although it is just another theory, it is possible that the fire in the O'Learys' barn started from the spontaneous combustion of hay. Barns where the hay is not kept perfectly dry can often burst into flames by spontaneous combustion. That is because wet hay is extremely prone to chemical decay. This chemical change can raise the temperature of the hay to its ignition point.

Fights broke out in saloons where men were trying to steal liquor. Then, less than three hours after the fire began, what may be the first violent death occurred. **Expressman** Jacob Klein was struck on the head with a shovel and killed by two men who stole the goods he was trying to save from a burning building.

By this time, the fire had traveled seven blocks northeast of the O'Learys' barn. Many firemen were already frustrated by their vain attempts to control the fire. Some gave up on fighting the fire and concentrated instead on rescuing people, helping them save their possessions, and even stopping looters.

Block after block of churches, factories, stores, houses, barns, and saloons were consumed by the flames. The only hope for stopping the rampaging fire was that it would not be able to jump the river. But the wind was blowing at 60 miles (96.5 kilometers) an hour, and it blew sparks not only across the river but also several blocks past it. Sometime around midnight, some of those embers settled on the Parmelee Stage and Omnibus Building three blocks east of the river, near Conley's Patch on the South Side. Soon the building was in flames, and the South Side was on fire.

The heart of Chicago was now in danger. The courthouse, the Tribune Building, the post office and customs house, the First National Bank, Tremont House, Crosby's Opera House, and most of Chicago's other large commercial and public buildings were crowded into the South Side, along with numerous mansions and churches. Fire engines rushed across the drawbridges from the West Side to protect them.

Conley's Patch disappeared in a **holocaust** of wind and fire shortly after 12:45 Monday morning. The intense heat of the fire caused buildings to disintegrate in minutes. Many residents were startled from their beds. Looking

confused and disheveled, they swarmed into the streets in panic, struggling with their meager possessions. Many of the Patch's lawbreakers took advantage of the disaster, robbing their fleeing neighbors, looting stores, and breaking into saloons to steal liquor. Some actually drank themselves into complete drunkenness and died in the fire.

Most of the Patch's refugees fled north toward the business district. The fire followed them, heading directly for the courthouse—and moving fast. Fiercely, it roared along the river. Flames enveloped everything along Market and Franklin Streets, including the city's gasworks and almost one hundred horses in John V. Farwell's express company barns. The heat was unbearable, and red fireworks made of sparks and debris lit up the sky. Every time the firefighters took a stand, the fire jumped over them, carried by the wind, and started another fire. They continued to fight, but it was hopeless. The fire could not be stopped.

It roared through buildings like a tornado, shot 100 feet (30 meters) into the air, and fell on roofs a block away. The wind whipped the flames away from one building, leaving it untouched, and deposited them on another.

In the basement of the courthouse, the jail cells were already full of smoke

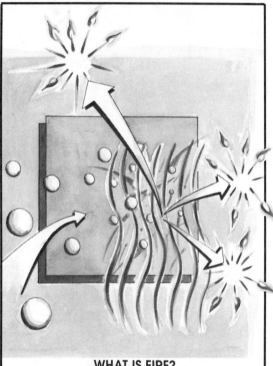

WHAT IS FIRE?

Fire is a chemical reaction that breaks material down and converts it into light and heat. The chemical reaction is known as combustion, and the material is called a *fuel*. In order for combustion to occur, the fuel must be exposed to two things: heat and oxygen.

Heat causes the *molecules*, or clusters of *atoms*, in the fuel to separate and move about rapidly. When the molecules reach an extremely high speed, they split into separate atoms, which are released into the air as gas. Oxygen in the air combines with this gas and causes small explosions. Fire is actually the heat and light from millions upon millions of these explosions.

when the more than one hundred terrified prisoners were finally released. One prisoner fainted, some stood in a daze, and others ran for safety.

By the time the courthouse was abandoned, the devastation was speeding east toward the mansions on Michigan Avenue. The gracious stone buildings of State Street, Crosby's Opera House, and the Tribune Building were directly in its path. *Tribune* co-publisher Joseph Medill ordered his employees to continue working on the newspaper as usual in the belief that his "fireproof" building would be safe.

However, at 3:00 Monday morning, he began to worry. He sent twenty men to the roof, and for four hours, they beat out the fires that started on the "fireproof" roofing material. The west side of the building grew so hot that windows cracked and the varnish on the office furniture smoked. By 7:00 A.M., Medill realized that the fight to save his building was lost, and he ordered his employees to evacuate.

As the pressman Conrad Kahler left the building, he met John McDevitt, a former **billiards** champion. McDevitt was headed toward Tom Foley's billiard parlor on Dearborn Street. Kahler warned him to get away, but McDevitt simply said, "Oh, the hell with you," and continued on. He died in the fire.

In a nearby building, a man stood in a fourth-floor window, about 50 feet (15 meters) above the sidewalk. In the street below, a crowd of people was yelling at him to jump. Suddenly the man disappeared from the window for a moment, and when he returned, he dropped a mattress down to the street. Slowly he backed out of the window, grasping the

window sill, and dropped to the third-floor window sill. As flames licked at his feet, he tried to swing from the window sill to the building next door, but it was too far. For a few tense moments, he hung there. Then he fell to the street. He was carried to Buck and Rayner's Drugstore, where he died a few minutes later.

All over the South Side, panicked people had fled from their homes and offices and jammed the streets, loading wagons, pushing wheelbarrows, carrying strong boxes, and carting books and baskets of laundry. Guests at the St. James Hotel, the Tremont House, and other downtown hotels threw their trunks out of windows and then jumped after them.

Many wagon drivers charged outrageous fees to haul people's belongings to a safe place. Some even dumped their loads just out of sight of the thankful customer and went looking for another victim to exploit. On the other hand, a number of drivers offered their service at regular rates or even for free. Rudolph Geiser, who owned a bird store on Randolph Street, turned down offers of twenty-five dollars and hauled loads free. He was so busy helping others that he had to hire a wagon to save his own goods.

Other citizens made valiant attempts to help, but, in the confusion, their efforts were misdirected. Elias R. Bowen, a store owner who sold military uniforms, thought he was being helpful when he rescued two horses from the flames. With great difficulty, he led them out of immediate danger and then wandered all over the city with them, trying to find a stable with empty stalls. When he finally found one, he left them and went directly to his place of business to try to save his own merchandise. The delay cost him fifteen thousand dollars worth of goods. In the meantime, firefighters on the steam engine *Long John* had been pulling the engine by hand all over the South Side because their horses had mysteriously disappeared.

In many areas, losing the horses wouldn't have mattered because the streets were too jammed with panicked people. Many adults held small children in their arms, while older children held

STARTING AND STOPPING FIRES

The minimum temperature at which substances will **ignite**, or begin to burn, is called the **ignition point**. Ignition points vary from substance to substance. Some materials, such as wood, coal, and hay, ignite at fairly low temperatures, which is why they make good fuel for fires. Other substances require such high temperatures to ignite that they eventually melt instead of bursting into flames. Some examples are stone and iron, which is why stone buildings are called fireproof.

Once a fire has been ignited, it will continue to burn until one of the three components of fire: fuel, heat, and oxygen, is removed. For example, when a fire reaches a cleared out area where no fuel is available, it will burn out. A fire can be extinguished before it runs out of fuel by pouring enough water on it to lower the temperature of the fuel below its ignition point. Chemicals and foam can also be used to extinguish fires. They attack fire by smothering the fuel, sealing out the oxygen required for combustion.

on tightly to their pets. Terrorized horses ran wildly through the crowds. The hot air was filled with the sounds of crying children, shouting drunks, barking dogs, roaring flames, crashing walls, and tugboats whistling as they pulled ships from the river to the safety of the lake.

Even in this bedlam, some people's reactions seem so strange they defy explanation. Solomon Witkowsky panicked when he saw the fire just a few blocks from his house on Third Avenue. He ran upstairs, got his revolver, and shot at the flames. Melville Stone was resting on the steps of the First National Bank on State Street shortly before it burned. A man sat down beside him and began cutting sheets of postage stamps into tiny pieces, then tossing them to the wind. "It seemed a perfectly natural thing to do," Stone said later.

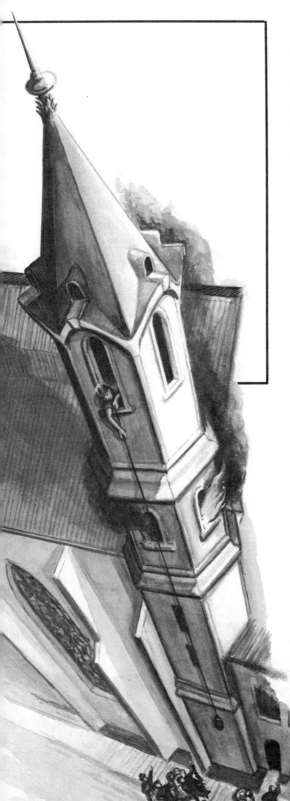

On Adams Street, rescuers forced a woman out of her home three times, and each time she ran back inside. She finally burned along with her possessions. The shouts of onlookers did not stop one man from running directly toward a burning building. He disappeared in a burst of flame before he reached the front door.

As the buildings in their path burned and collapsed one by one, the flames leapt north and east, and then south. Shortly after noon on Monday, the fire had traveled far enough south to reach the tower of the Wabash Avenue Methodist Church.

William Haskell, a former professional gymnast, was determined to save the church. Carrying a long, sturdy rope, he climbed by ladder to the roof of the church 75 feet (22.5 meters) above the ground. He hauled up bucketful after bucketful of water to wet down the roof and himself, beating out sparks all the while. Then he climbed to the top of the 100-foot (30 meter) tower and fastened the rope to it. Grabbing a bucket of water, Haskell lowered himself down inside the tower. After a long absence, he reappeared, took another bucket, and disappeared inside again.

After several more trips, the fire in the tower was out. Haskell was declared the hero of the South Side by the watching crowd. They even took up a collection to reward him, but the collectors disappeared with the money. Nevertheless, William Haskell had not only saved the church, but he had prevented the fire from spreading any further south.

Four
The Path of the Fire

Although William Haskell helped stop the fire from spreading in one direction, firefighters were having little success elsewhere. As the West Side and South Side went up in flames, many residents fled to the North Side, where they thought they would be safe.

A few adventurous people, however, did not flee. One of these was Alexander Frear, a New York politician who was visiting his family in Chicago. While checking on the safety of his relatives, Frear managed to follow the fire's progress through the city. His story, published in the October 15, 1871, issue of the *New York World*, is one of the most thorough eyewitness accounts of the fire.

At about 11:00 P.M. Frear was at the Sherman House on the South Side looking for friends when he heard about the fire. His brother's house was on Ewing Street in the West Side, just four blocks from the O'Learys' barn. Since his brother was out of town, Frear set out immediately for the West Side to make sure the rest of the family was safe:

I ran as fast as I could to the Adams Street bridge. Vehicles and people were streaming in from all the streets to the west. I paid little attention to anything, my anxiety to reach my sister's house being very great. With difficulty I got to the bridge, . . . where tugs were screaming to get through. There was much confusion, and suddenly a rush of people made toward me as the bridge began to swing, and I ran to get over.

When he finally reached the house, he found Mrs. Frear and her three children safe. All three of the children were under 15, and the youngest, Johnny, was crippled. So she asked Frear to take the children to her friends, the Kimballs, on the South Side, where she thought they would be safer. He had no sooner returned from that errand than he and Mrs. Frear learned that the fire had already spread into the Kimballs' neighborhood:

> *I begged Mrs. Frear not to alarm herself, and ran up to the roof. The house was a two-story-and-a-half frame building, but it joined another which was an addition to a lumber mill. I clambered to the roof of the latter, and was nearly swept off by the wind…. Wherever I could see at all the wind blew the burning houses into a mass of live coals that was dazzling.*

Frear and his sister-in-law, determined to find the children, struggled west on foot to Halsted Street. There they finally found a cab that took them on a roundabout route to the intersection of Washington Street and Wabash Avenue on the South Side before a police officer stopped them:

> *In the confusion it was difficult to get any information; but I was told that the block in which the Kimballs lived was burning, and that the people were all out. To add to my distress, Mrs. Frear jumped out of the vehicle and started to run in the direction of the fire. Nothing, I am satisfied, saved her from being crushed to death in a mad attempt to find her children but for the appearance of an acquaintance, who told her that the children were all safe at the St. James Hotel.*

They fought their way to the St. James on the corner of Washington and State Streets, but the children were not there, so Frear left Mrs. Frear at the hotel and went to look for them:

I then ran as fast as I could through Randolph Street to Sherman House, thinking we might have mistaken the hotel.... The corridor was a scene of intense excitement. The guests of the house were running about wildly, some of them dragging their trunks to the stairway. Everything was in confusion.... I looked out of one of the south windows of the house, and shall never forget the terribly magnificent sight I saw. The courthouse park was filled with people, who appeared to be huddled together in a solid mass, helpless and astounded. The whole air was filled with the falling cinders, and it looked like a snowstorm lit by colored fire.

In the hotel, Frear met another nephew who asked him if he wanted to see the fire, and they set off in a wagon, stopping soon at Wright's Cafe on Wabash Avenue to get a cup of coffee:

There were several of the firemen of the Little Giant in there. One of the men was bathing his head with whisky from a flask. They declared that the entire department had given up, overworked, and that they could do nothing more.

Frear and his nephew then drove down Wabash Avenue:

> *Looking back..., I saw the smoke and flames pouring out...from the very point we had just left, and the intervening space was filled with the whirling embers that beat against the houses and covered the roofs and windowsills. It seemed like a tornado of fire. To add to the terror, animals, burnt and infuriated by the cinders, darted through the streets regardless of all human obstacles.*
>
> *We then hurried on toward the St. James Hotel, passing through some of the strangest and saddest scenes it has ever been my misfortune to witness. I saw a woman kneeling in the street with a crucifix held up before her and the skirt of her dress burning while she prayed. We had barely passed before a runaway truck dashed her to the ground.*

THE PATH OF THE FIRE

1. At approximately 9:00 P.M Sunday, October 8, the fire begins on the West Side in the O'Learys' barn at 137 De Koven Street. The fire was under control on the West Side at about 3:00 P.M Monday.

2. At about midnight Sunday night, it jumps the river to the South Side and burns the Parmelee Stage and Omnibus Building at Franklin and Jackson Streets.

3. The fire consumes Conley's Patch and heads toward downtown and the courthouse at La Salle and Washington Streets. At 3:00 A.M. Monday, the courthouse collapses.

4. At 2:30 A.M. Monday, it crosses the river to the North Side near the State Street Bridge. Shortly after 3:00 A.M., the waterworks catches on fire and collapses an hour later.

5. The fire spreads north, east, and west throughout the North Side.

6. The fire is still raging near Lincoln Park when rain starts at 11:00 P.M. Monday, October 9. Thanks to the rain, the fire is stopped just north of Fullerton Avenue, about twenty-six hours after it began.

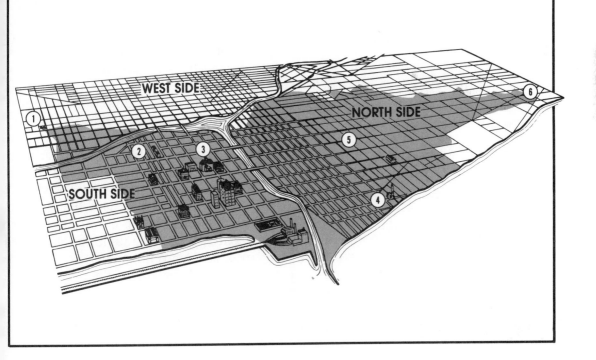

When they returned to the St. James Hotel, between 2:00 and 3:00 on Monday morning, they learned that Mrs. Frear had been taken to a friend's house on the North Side. But the hotel was still full of terrified people:

> *Women and children were screaming, and baggage was being thrown about in the most reckless manner. I now concluded Mrs. Frear's children had been lost....*
>
> *Finally word was brought that the bridges were burning, and all escape was cut off to the north and west. Then ensued a scene which was beyond description. Men shouted the news and added to the panic. Women, half-dressed, and many of them with screaming children, fled out of the building. There was a jam in the doorway, and they struck and clawed each other as if in self-defense. I lost sight of my nephew at this time.*

Frear then left the St. James to walk back to his sister's house:

> *I went through to Wabash Avenue, and here the thoroughfare was utterly choked with all manner of goods and people. Everybody who had been forced from the other end of town by the advancing flames had brought some article with him, and, as further progress was delayed, if not completely stopped by the river—the bridges of which were also choked—most of them, in their panic, abandoned their burdens, so that the streets and sidewalks presented the most astonishing wreck. Valuable oil paintings, books, pet animals, musical instruments, toys, mirrors, and bedding, were trampled underfoot.*

When Frear finally arrived at his sister's house, he found the fire had passed it by. There he met his nephew, who informed him that Mrs. Frear was safe in a house on the North Side. Exhausted, Frear lay down in the hallway and went to sleep.

Only a half hour later, at about 3:00 Monday morning, he was awakened with the news that Mrs. Frear was again in danger. By then the courthouse had collapsed in rubble, sending fiery, airborne embers onto the State Street Bridge. He ran toward the North Side to rescue her. From there, Frear saw this somber scene:

> *We could see across the river at the cross streets in the South Side that where yesterday was a populous city was now a mass of smoking ruins. All the way round we encountered thousands of people; but the excitement had given way to a terrible grief and desolation.*

By the time they found Mrs. Frear, the North Side was in chaos, but Frear managed to get a wagon and take her home. At 4:00 that afternoon, they learned that the children were safe with the Kimballs on the outskirts of the city.

One reason for the chaos in the North Side was that many residents waited until the last minute to flee the fire. The homes of the wealthy and middle-class people who lived there were not crowded so closely together. Also, nearly all the factories, lumberyards, and warehouses were situated along the river banks. Therefore, most North Side residents who were awake and knew about the fire were confident that it would be controlled before it reached their neighborhoods.

This illustration first appeared in *Harper's Weekly* on October 28, 1871.

Early Monday morning, however, the rampaging flames were consuming the wooden houses, barns, sidewalks, fences, and trees on the North Side, speeding across withered grass and dry, fallen leaves. The wind whipped through the open land and between the houses, fanning the fire steadily northward. Many people were asleep and knew nothing about the fire until neighbors and friends shouted and banged on their doors to awaken them. Then all they could do was dress hurriedly and flee for their lives.

Mahlon Ogden was one of the few people on the North Side brave enough to fight the fire and try to save his home. When the fire reached the Ogdens' residence, which occupied an entire block on Lafayette Place, their three-story house was crowded with North Side residents who had already abandoned their homes. Wagons, furniture, cows, and horses filled the grounds. Ogden and his friends hung wet carpets on the sides of the house and barn, while other friends poured water on the roof and swept off the sparks. They fought for hours, and then, just when all seemed lost, the wind died down, making the fire easier to control. When the wind rose again, it blew the flames away from the house.

The Ogdens' home was one of only two homes saved in the entire burned-out section of the North Side. The other was the cottage of Richard Bellinger, a newly married policeman who lived on Lincoln Place, near Lincoln Park. On

THE STEAMER

A nineteenth-century steamer, drawn by galloping horses, was quite a sight. Steamers careened down the streets, with clouds of steam and cinders hissing noisily from their boiler stacks. Wood or coal was burned in the steamer's upright boiler made of glistening brass and nickel, which produced steam to drive a pump.

The intake pipe, which had two or more outlets for hoses, was attached to a hydrant, and the pump forced the water through the hoses. This equipment was mounted on a brightly painted, four-wheel carriage. In addition to a number, every engine had a name, such as *Winnebago*, *Long John*, or *Little Giant*.

Monday afternoon, while the flames roared through the North Side directly toward his small, white cottage, he and his brother-in-law raked up the leaves in the yard. They also removed the fence, the front steps, and the wooden sidewalk. They covered the roof with wet carpets and placed buckets of water all around the house. Then they stood guard, putting out sparks for hours until the fire had passed them by.

Most North Side residents, however, abandoned their homes to the fire after trying to save as many possessions as possible. They carried their belongings out to the streets, where they fought to hire one of the few, unloaded wagons that passed by. Soon wagons drawn by frightened horses and loaded with furniture, clothing, paintings, and cooking pots, were skidding crazily through the streets.

Families and their servants scurried toward safety, covering their heads to protect themselves from flying embers and scorching heat. Some families fled to the prairies on the western outskirts of the city, where they congregated in makeshift camps. Others headed north to Lincoln Park.

The new waterworks was destroyed in less than an hour.

But people who lived in the southeast corner of the North Side were cut off from safety by the line of fire. Panic stricken, they ran from one street to another, trying to find a way to escape, but the wall of flames had trapped them. In desperation, they gathered on the Sands, a lakefront beach just north of the river. Thousands of terrified people, along with hundreds of pets and barn animals, crowded onto the beach. Some sat on the ground hanging on to feather beds, others sat on trunks full of money and valuable goods. Mothers nursed babies, and children cuddled pets. A young girl burst into tears because her canary had dropped dead in its cage. In the confusion, thieves looted trunks in plain sight of the dazed owners. Some men buried their wives and children in wet sand, leaving only small holes for air, to protect them from the heat and flying sparks.

To the panicked residents, the wind and fire appeared to be a single raging demon, alive with evil intent. Shortly after 3:00 A.M., this demon performed the most damaging act imaginable. It blew a blazing piece of timber onto the waterworks. In spite of the desperate efforts of assistant engineer Francis Trautman and his men to save it, the

waterworks was destroyed in less than an hour.

Only the isolated water tower remained. Soon the fire hoses, held by weary, despairing firefighters, sputtered and went dry all over the city. Without water, the fight against the fire was lost. Many of the firemen gave up.

By Monday night, Lincoln Park and Cemetery was temporary shelter for about thirty thousand homeless men, women, and children. Still the fire continued its march along the west side of the park, consuming fences, trees, stacks of furniture, and personal belongings that people had brought from their homes. Huddled together, the refugees in the park sang and prayed.

Then, at 11:00 P.M., Monday, October 9, 1871, the drought that had created the severe fire conditions ended. Cold rain began to fall, slowly halting the march of the fire. The last home burned by the Great Chicago Fire was owned by John A. Huck. It was on the north side of Fullerton Avenue, just north of Lincoln Park.

For twenty-six hours, the fire had ravaged the city. In a path almost 1 mile (1.6 kilometers) wide, the flames had marched 4 miles (6.4 kilometers) from the O'Learys' barn on the West Side to John Huck's house on the North Side. Three and a half square miles (5 square kilometers) of the city had been destroyed. In the end, approximately 250 people were killed, 98,500 people were homeless, and 17,450 buildings were destroyed.

By late Monday afternoon, the fire had consumed most of the *fuel* within its reach and was no longer spreading. It would be many days before all the pockets of fire stopped smoldering, but at least Chicago's citizens no longer had to fear the flames.

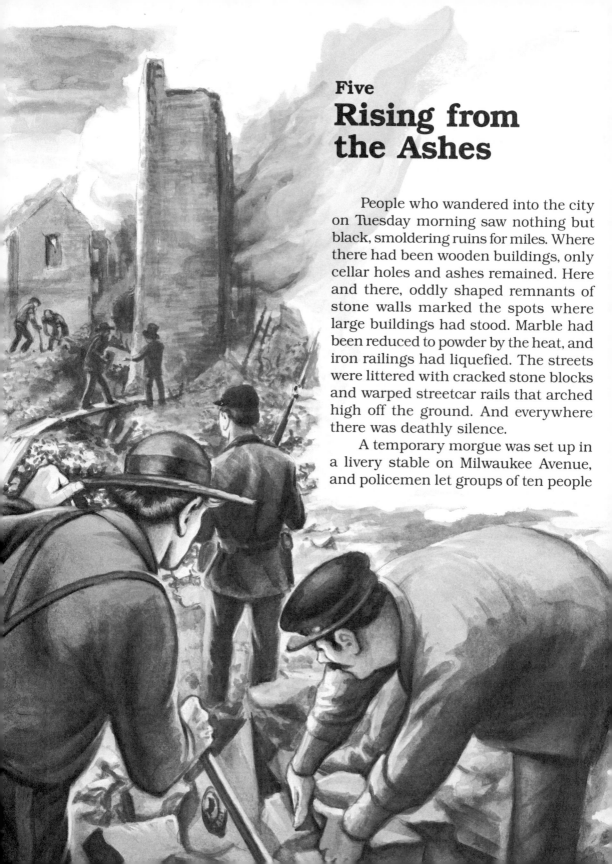

Five
Rising from the Ashes

People who wandered into the city on Tuesday morning saw nothing but black, smoldering ruins for miles. Where there had been wooden buildings, only cellar holes and ashes remained. Here and there, oddly shaped remnants of stone walls marked the spots where large buildings had stood. Marble had been reduced to powder by the heat, and iron railings had liquefied. The streets were littered with cracked stone blocks and warped streetcar rails that arched high off the ground. And everywhere there was deathly silence.

A temporary morgue was set up in a livery stable on Milwaukee Avenue, and policemen let groups of ten people in at a time to identify bodies, many of which were burned beyond recognition. The official estimate of the death toll was between 200 and 300, although only 120 bodies were found. An accurate count was impossible. Some people left the city during the fire and never returned. Many bodies were doubtless consumed completely by the flames. Other victims disappeared into the river and were never found, and many of the hapless residents of Conley's Patch had no friends or relatives to report them missing.

As the survivors began to sift through the ashes, they found odd relics of the disaster. One report claims that from over a million books in Booksellers' Row on State Street, only one legible page was left unburned. It was from a Bible and contained the following verse from the first chapter of the Lamentations of Jeremiah: "How doth the city sit solitary, that was full of people! how is she become as a widow! she that was great among the nations.... She weepeth sore in the night, and her tears are on her cheeks."

The city was not entirely solitary when the people returned on Tuesday morning. Against all odds, at least two animals survived. In the ruins of the post office, in a half-filled bucket of water, sat the post office cat. And a huge St. Bernard, which was left every night inside the fireproof vault of the Fidelity Safe Deposit Insurance Company to guard the money, barked with relief when the vault was opened.

Oddly enough, although 17,500 buildings in the path of the fire were destroyed, a few remained either partially or completely intact. The North

THE DAY AFTER

Many photographs such as this were taken of Chicago the day after the Great Fire. So it is puzzling that not a single photograph of the fire itself exists. It could be that the fire moved so quickly, the bulky, slow equipment could not operate fast enough, or that the cameras, and the photographers, could not function in the suffocating heat. It is also possible that any pictures taken during the fire were burned. No one knows for certain.

Side homes of Mahlon Ogden and Richard Bellinger stood as symbols of their owners' defiance of the flames. An entire block of buildings at the corner of Market and Randolph Streets on the South Side survived, as did three buildings in Lincoln Park. And the water tower on the North Side was still standing. Oddest of all, the cottage of Patrick and Catherine O'Leary, just 40 feet (12 meters) from the barn where the fire started, survived completely intact.

A complete list of destroyed buildings was never made. The people of Chicago were too busy with restoring order, helping the homeless refugees, and rebuilding their city.

Even on Monday afternoon, while the fire was still raging, Mayor Roswell B. Mason began issuing proclamations to keep order in the city. Many citizens were worried that crime would increase as a result of the fire. They formed a delegation that persuaded Mayor Mason and General Philip Sheridan, a former Civil War hero, to put the city under **martial law**, giving the military forces temporary authority to enforce laws. The soldiers on duty in the city were unpopular with many of the residents, especially when they misused their authority.

Martial law was becoming increasingly controversial when an incident took place on October 18 that resolved the issue. Colonel Thomas W. Grosvenor, the city prosecutor who had been a leading proponent of martial law, was walking home from a party when a young soldier asked, "Who goes there?"

"SHOOT TO KILL"

The Pinkerton Detective Agency, founded in the early 1850s by Allan Pinkerton, a Scottish immigrant to Chicago, was one of the first private detective agencies in the country. Immediately after the fire, the city hired the Pinkerton men to patrol the burnt-out business district.

On Monday, October 9, 1871, Pinkerton issued the following proclamation to his men:

Grosvenor refused to stop or answer, so the soldier threatened to shoot. Grosvenor yelled back, "Go ahead and bang away!" The soldier did, and Grosvenor died of the wound. On October 23, the controversial martial law ended.

Another serious problem was the plight of the 98,500 people left homeless by the fire. About two-thirds of them had no place to go. On Monday, October 9, a relief headquarters was set up in the First Congregational Church, and relief

stations where the homeless could go for information, food, and supplies appeared quickly all over Chicago. Other cities responded generously to Chicago's needs with trainloads of food and clothing. By late Tuesday, ten carloads of bread, fowl, crackers, flour, sugar, beef, pork, coffee, doughnuts, cheese, cake, fruit, and cabbage had been handed out. Financial contributions totaling almost five million dollars poured in from the United States and twenty-nine foreign countries.

Many con artists tried taking advantage of the generosity extended to Chicago's refugees by every city in the country. Hoping for handouts, they posed in other cities as refugees from the fire, prompting a Philadelphia newspaper to report:

Chicago was probably the most populous city in the world previous to the conflagration. Some 14,000,000 of her "destitute citizens" have passed through this city in the past three weeks. You can't throw a cat in any direction without hitting a "sufferer."

While a few Chicago merchants tried to profit from the disaster by charging exorbitant prices for food, water, and rentals, most showed genuine compassion. Pat O'Connell, for example, posted a sign outside his West Side grocery store that said, "All Parties Without Money Can Have Meat Here."

By Monday afternoon, the Chicago newspapers had found temporary headquarters and begun publishing again. Soon they were full of lost and found ads, including this one: "Mr. McLogan, 288 Laflin, has a boy 2 or 3 years old—speaks French." Another one read: "Will the gentlemen who gave me the clock and picture on State st. Oct. 9 call at 258 Cottage Grove av. Dr. Steere."

The city was destroyed, but the spirit of its residents scarcely faltered. "CHEER UP," said an editorial in the *Chicago Tribune* on Wednesday:

In the midst of a calamity without parallel in the world's history, looking upon the ashes of thirty years' accumulations, the people of this once beautiful city have resolved that CHICAGO SHALL RISE AGAIN.

All day Tuesday, October 10, small fires burned in pockets throughout the city, and, for days afterwards, fires smoldered in coal piles and basements. But the people of Chicago paid them no heed. The first load of lumber arrived on the South Side Tuesday afternoon, and workers began tearing down the ruins before the bricks had even cooled. Businesses were set up in houses, churches, and basements. Temporary signs were tacked up throughout the city. Sign-painters Moore and Goes left a sign giving their new address on the West Side. Underneath the address was painted: "*Capital, $000,000.30.*"

Schock, Bigford & Company was the first business opened after the fire. For a total investment of $2.50, they set up a stand on Dearborn Street opposite the ruins of the post office. Here they sold cigars, tobacco, grapes, apples, and cider. On the morning of Tuesday, October 10, W.D. Kerfoot, a real estate dealer, put up the first new building, a 12-by-16-foot (3.6-by-4.8 meter) shack, in the business district. His sign announced, "ALL GONE BUT WIFE, CHILDREN & ENERGY."

Few Chicago businessmen were as eager or as daring to begin anew as was John Drake, owner of the Tremont House Hotel. Moments after his hotel was destroyed on Monday, the ninth, Drake walked into the Michigan Avenue Hotel ten blocks away and offered the owner one thousand dollars for it. With flames raging just a block away, the owner thought he was crazy but gladly sold it to him. After the fire, the Michigan was still standing, virtually unharmed. Its former owner tried to back out of the deal, but Drake insisted. He renamed it the Tremont House and opened almost immediately.

The sixty-five thousand homeless refugees, most of them from the poor working classes, were not so fortunate. They crowded into tents and temporary barracks, and a month after the fire, sixty thousand of them were still on relief. On the whole, however, relocation moved faster than anyone expected. The relief society gave away lumber for one-room houses, and every single piece of usable material was salvaged from the ruins. A week after the fire, 5,497 temporary buildings had been built, and 200 permanent buildings were under construction. Within three months, 6,000 small shacks, 2,000 permanent wooden structures, and 500 brick or stone buildings were completed or nearly completed.

Despite their desire to build a better, more fireproof city after the Great Fire, the city fathers also recognized that thousands of refugees needed shelter immediately. The quickest way to construct new buildings was with wood. Within months, Chicago was again crowded with wooden houses and other buildings. Some reflective residents realized that, in its haste, Chicago had once again made itself a target for fiery disaster.

William Croffut, managing editor of the *Chicago Evening Post*, made this impassioned plea for discontinuing the use of wood for building:

There is scarcely any city on the continent so exposed to prolonged and terrible winds as Chicago. Our constant imminent menace is that autumnal southwest hurricane which sweeps up from the wide prairie to the lake, eager to seize upon a spark and nurse it into a conflagration.... Nothing but acres of solid brick, or stone buildings that are virtually fireproof can stop it.

View from Cook County Courthouse after the fire.

Six
The Battle Against City Fire

To this day, the cause of the Great Fire remains unknown. All that is known for certain is that it started in the O'Learys' barn at approximately 9:00 P.M. on Sunday, October 8, 1871. The city's official inquiry into the cause of the blaze was inconclusive, so many people developed their own theories.

Popular legend holds that the Great Chicago Fire began when Mrs. O'Leary went into the barn to milk a cow, and the cow kicked over her lantern. Although the facts clearly show otherwise, newspaper reporters and gossips of the day were not convinced, so Catherine O'Leary has gone down in history as the person who started the great disaster.

Much of the publicity about Mrs. O'Leary was probably an example of anti-Irish sentiment. Outrageous newspaper accounts in the days immedi-

ately following the disaster indignantly depicted her as a drunk, a withered old hag, or a witch.

Even so, not everyone believed that Mrs. O'Leary was responsible. In fact, several theories arose to explain the cause of the fire, all equally implausible. For example, there were those who believed that God had started the fire to punish Chicago for its evil ways. Others claimed that a fire-extinguisher salesman had set it to prove how much Chicago needed his product. Still others believed that the O'Learys' tenants, the McLaughlins, had gone into the barn to get milk for a party punch and accidentally knocked over their lantern.

Although the immediate cause of the fire that started in the O'Learys' barn will never be known, it is not surprising that a fire did start in Chicago on the night of October 8, 1871. Unseasonably warm weather, a lack of rain, and the wind had left the city dangerously dry. In the slums and lower-class neighborhoods, the crowded, wooden houses, barns, and industrial plants had become excellent fuel for a fire. In fact, twenty-seven fires had broken out earlier that week in the tinder-dry city.

Because Chicago was plagued with fire even before the Great Fire, many building owners had attempted to make their buildings fireproof by constructing them of bricks or stone. Almost every one of these "fireproof" structures was destroyed by the fire in 1871. Among them was the luxurious, new Grand Pacific Hotel, which was still under construction on October 8. The Grand Pacific boasted an innovative fire-prevention system made up of huge water tanks installed beneath the roof. In case of fire, the water could be dropped quickly into the building. Unfortunately for the Grand Pacific, its tanks had not yet been filled with water when the fire struck.

MRS. O'LEARY'S COMET

In 1985, 114 years after the fire, a man named Mel Waskin published a book entitled *Mrs. O'Leary's Comet!* In it, he theorizes that the fire was caused when Biela's Comet collided with Earth. His theory is based primarily on three pieces of evidence.

First, scientists in the nineteenth century had charted the comet's path and believed that it had been on a collision course with Earth since 1832. It was last seen in the 1840s, and then it disappeared forever. Waskin believes that the comet actually collided with the earth on the night of the Chicago Fire.

Second, the comet had a long, two-pronged tail. According to Waskin's theory, these prongs hit the earth hundreds of miles north of Chicago, causing two other disastrous fires that broke out on the same night in Michigan and Wisconsin.

Third, Waskin points out how incredibly intense the heat of the fire was. It was so hot that it burned large buildings to the ground in minutes, even melting stone and iron. Waskin maintains that even high winds could not account for such an *inferno*. Instead, only the gases in the comet could have burned with the kind of heat associated with the Chicago Fire.

Waskin's theory is interesting, but it does not explain how a comet could have landed inside the O'Learys' small barn without destroying it instantly. Or why Daniel Sullivan, who was able to rescue the calf from the O'Learys' barn, did not see or hear an explosion. Finally, Waskin does not explain how a comet streaking through the sky above Chicago could have gone unnoticed by 300,000 people.

This 1871 engraving shows the prejudice of many who accused Mrs. O'Leary of starting the fire.

Photo courtesy of Chicago Historical Society.

After the fire, architects and builders continued to experiment with new ways to protect buildings from fire. One builder, for example, designed attached houses that had double walls between them with a 4-inch (10 centimeter) space that could be filled with water in case of fire. During the Great Chicago Fire, Architect John Mills Van Osdel, who had designed the Palmer House Hotel, accidently discovered another fire-safety technique. When he realized the hotel was doomed, he buried his important papers in a pit in the hotel basement and covered them with 2 feet (.6 meters) of wet sand, topped with a layer of clay. The clay baked in the fire and preserved the papers, which led to the use of clay tiles for fireproofing. While many residents supported these

efforts to make the city safer from the risks of fire, corruption, greed, and ignorance often stood in their way.

City leaders knew, for example, that building a paint and varnish factory next to a lumber mill full of wood and sawdust was inviting a disaster. However, if they were paid a high enough bribe, they were willing to overlook the danger. Laws were passed to regulate what could be built on lots in certain areas, to mandate the proper storage of hazardous materials, and to restrict the use of wood for building. Nevertheless, violations were common and usually went unpunished.

One month after the Great Fire, Joseph Medill was elected mayor by campaigning on the "fireproof" ticket. He quickly pushed a bill through the city council forbidding wooden buildings in the burned-out area of Chicago. Even as that law was being passed, however, the city's Board of Public Works was issuing one-year permits for temporary, one- or two-story, wooden buildings in the same area. People's need for housing and other buildings was greater than their fear of another fire. Therefore,

wood construction continued.

In the late nineteenth century, Chicago was not the only American city constantly threatened by fire. Almost every major American city, including Boston, New York City, St. Louis, and San Francisco, endured at least one large **urban** fire before the turn of the century. Until the Great Chicago Fire, the lessons learned in those fires were often quickly forgotten. Even worse, the lessons learned by one city after a fire were not heeded by other cities. Like the residents of Chicago, people in each city believed that "it couldn't happen here." But the Great Chicago Fire changed that. Its intensity and devastation captured the attention of the entire nation and underscored the need for improved fire safety.

It was the country's insurance companies that first saw the problem on a nationwide scale and acted to combat it. They had reason to be concerned. After the Great Fire, most insurance companies suffered great losses, and many were forced out of business. And, since the cities were slow to pass and enforce fire safety laws, the insurance compa-

nies decided to take the matter into their own hands.

In 1873, the National Board of Fire Underwriters, a nationwide organization that handled public service activities for the insurance industry, called for a number of fire safety laws that would benefit the whole country. A special committee of the board, which had studied Chicago extensively, warned the city about its continued fire hazards. It recommended that Chicago enforce more restrictive building regulations and expand the fire department and water supply facilities. It also recommended Chicago create a fire marshall's bureau and establish a plan for gradually removing specific fire hazards. In spite of these recommendations, the city failed to pass stricter regulations or even enforce existing ones.

As a result, on July 14, 1874, a fire started just blocks from the O'Leary cottage. Before it was brought under control, it destroyed eight hundred wooden buildings, with losses totaling three million dollars. This time the National Board of Fire Underwriters demanded that the city council enforce its own 1871 law forbidding wooden buildings in the area burned out by the Great Chicago Fire. It also demanded that the council act on the board's 1873 recommendations for stricter fire safety codes. At first, the city council refused to meet these demands, so all the insurance offices in town closed their doors. After two months, the council agreed to take action, and the offices reopened.

The Great Fire of 1871 also prompted the fire chiefs in fifty of America's major cities to act. In October 1873, they formed the association now known as the International Association of Fire Chiefs. Although they did nothing grand or dramatic, the fire chiefs worked hard to improve fire prevention and fire fighting techniques. They persuaded manufacturers of hoses and other fire-fighting equipment to standardize sizes and parts so that cities could lend each other equipment in emergencies. By the early twentieth century, fire chiefs were conducting fire inspections in business and industrial sites. In some cities, they began inspecting homes and apartments for fire hazards such as faulty electrical wiring, inflammable materials stored near furnaces, and insufficient fire escapes.

But progress was slow. Often fire hazards were not regulated until after a disastrous fire. In 1903, a fire in the Iroquois Theater in Chicago killed 575 people. After that disaster, the city acted quickly to impose stricter fire regulations on theaters. Fire-resistant curtains, additional exits, and automatic fire sprinklers all became mandatory.

Furthermore, new construction methods and technology were constantly creating new fire hazards. Skyscrapers, for example, were built much higher than fire hoses could shoot water. Regulations had to be passed requiring water storage tanks in all buildings over six stories high. These tanks, similar to those first used in Chicago's Grand Pacific Hotel in 1871, are still the main defense against fire in skyscrapers. Now, however, the tanks are connected to automatic sprinklers in

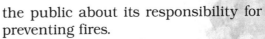

the public about its responsibility for preventing fires.

Of course, fire safety is only half the battle against fire. Once a fire starts, the firefighters must be able to control it quickly and safely. Over the years, fire fighting was also made more effective through the introduction of innovative equipment and techniques.

every room, as well as to valves and hoses on every floor.

Although the struggle to improve fire safety was slow, it was successful. Rarely since 1910 has an urban fire raged out of control. That is due in large part to strict laws. The construction and use of public buildings are carefully regulated by local, state, and national fire laws. Portable fire extinguishers, smoke alarms, and automatic sprinkler systems are required by law in most public buildings.

Fire inspectors regularly check to see that fire doors operate correctly, that hazardous materials are properly stored, or that the number of people in a public building does not exceed the allowable occupancy rate. And all large fire departments have fire prevention bureaus whose main task is to educate

If the Great Chicago Fire were to start in the O'Learys' barn today, its story would be very different. The differences would begin as soon as Daniel Sullivan spotted the flames bursting out of the O'Learys' barn. Here is what might have happened next:

Running inside his house to his telephone, Sullivan quickly dials 911 and reports the fire. Within forty-five seconds, firefighters are on their way to the O'Learys' house. Sirens screaming, the powerful trucks move quickly through the crowded city streets, and help arrives at 137 De Koven Street within minutes.

The **pumpers** arrive first. They have powerful pumps that can propel water through their hoses at 1,500 gallons (5,685 liters) per minute and carry their own water supply in 500-gallon (1,900 liter) tanks. While some firefighters quickly attach a hose to the nearest fire hydrant, others are already surrounding the barn and dousing the

fire with water from the pumpers' tanks. Because they are wearing special protective helmets, fire coats, and boots, they can work close to the fire and direct the water where it is most needed. It is too late to save the barn, so a number of firefighters begin wetting down the nearby houses.

In the meantime, the station commanders check to make sure no people are in immediate danger. Quickly, they investigate the scene, communicating on their walkie-talkies as they **size up** the situation and devise their battle plan. Because none of the buildings in the block are over two stories tall, they decide they do not need an **aerial ladder truck**. They also do not need **crash trucks**, which carry both foam-making and dry chemicals used to smother gasoline, electrical, and oil fires. **Fireboats**, capable of pumping 22,000 gallons (83,600 liters) of water per minute, are on the river, too far away to help.

Suddenly a commander notices that the Dalton's house near the barn is

smoldering. "Go *ventilate* that house," he yells. Quickly two firemen run to the house and break several windows. By ventilating, or creating openings in the house through which heat, smoke, and toxic gases can escape, the firefighters prevent an explosion from the pressure that would otherwise build up inside.

The flames damage the Dalton's house and the one beside it, but soon the fire is extinguished. Most of the pumpers return to their stations, but one remains behind so the firefighters can *overhaul* the site of the fire. Carefully, they sift through the ashes of the barn and check hidden areas in the nearby houses to make sure the fire is out. Once certain that it is, the firefighters begin their *salvage* work, mopping up water inside the buildings and covering the broken windows with plastic sheeting. Then they repack their gear on the pumper and leave.

Although it would be little consolation to the unfortunate residents of Chicago who suffered in the Great Fire that began on October 8, 1871, it is true that the lessons learned from that fiery disaster have benefited all Americans since. Those lessons spurred the growth and improvement of the fire safety practices and fire fighting techniques that make an urban fire on the scale of the Great Fire practically impossible in America today.

Glossary

aerial ladder truck .....A large fire engine that carries folding ladders.

atom ....The smallest basic part of any material thing. One or more atoms make up a molecule.

billiards ....[**BIL**-yerds] A game very similar to pool, played on a table with balls and a cue stick.

combustible.................Capable of burning.

combustion..................The process of burning; a chemical reaction that converts fuel to heat.

crash truck ....A specially-equipped fire engine that carries chemicals used to control oil, gasoline, and electrical fires.

crib ....A house or room at the mouth of a water intake system and containing filtering equipment.

expressman ....A delivery man who hauls freight with horses and a wagon.

fireboat ....A boat equipped with pumps and hoses, which uses water from the river, lake, or bay to put out fires.

flammable ....Combustible. Capable of being set on fire.

fuel ....Any material that burns.

grain elevator ....A building used to store grain. It contains machinery for loading and unloading the grain.

holocaust ....[**HALL**-uh-cost] A great or total destruction of people or places by some disaster such as fire or war.

horsecars ....Streetcars that run on rails and are drawn by horses.

hose elevator ....A fire engine with a movable platform that lifts firefighters up so they can direct water to the upper stories of a building.

ignite...........................To set on fire, to begin to burn.

ignition point ....The lowest temperature at which a material will burst into flames.

immigrant....................A person who moves to a new country with the intention of living there permanently.

inferno ....Another name for hell, commonly used to describe a large fire.

jackscrew ....A hand-operated jack for lifting heavy objects a short distance off the ground.

land speculator ....A person who buys land and holds on to it until it increases in value and can be sold for a profit.

martial law ....An emergency situation in which the state or national military comes in to enforce the law in an area where civil obedience has broken down.

molecule ....[**MOL**-i-cyool] In chemistry, the smallest particle of a substance that can exist alone without losing its form. Molecules are made of one or more atoms.

overhaul ....The fire-fighting procedure for making sure a fire is out. Firemen sift through ashes and thoroughly check the entire area of the fire.

portage ....An overland route that is used to carry boats and goods between two bodies of water.

pumper ....A fire engine that has powerful pumps, long hoses, and its own limited water supply in a tank.

salvage ....The clean-up procedure in which firefighters reduce the damage they have caused at the site of a fire. It includes such tasks as mopping up excess water and covering broken windows with plastic.

size up ....The investigative method that fire commanders use when they arrive at the scene of a fire to determine the nature of the fire and the best way to fight it.

smolder ....To burn and smoke without flame.

steamer ....A fire engine pulled by horses. Features a steam engine to pump the water through the hoses.

underworld ....The criminal culture of a society.

urban.............................Having to do with cities or towns.

ventilate ....The procedure in which firefighters break windows or chop holes in a wall to prevent heat and gas from building up inside a structure and causing an explosion.

Further Reading

THE GREAT CHICAGO FIRE

Kogan, Herman, and Robert Cromie. *The Great Fire: Chicago, 1871*. New York: G.P. Putnam's Sons, 1971.

Lowe, David. *The Great Chicago Fire: In Eyewitness Accounts and 70 Contemporary Photographs and Illustrations*. New York: Dover Publications, Inc., 1979.

FIRE AND FIRE FIGHTING

Blumberg, Rhoda. *Firefighters*. New York: Franklin Watts, 1976.

Colby, C.B. *Space Age Fire Fighters: New Weapons in the Fireman's Arsenal*. New York: Coward, McCann & Geoghegan, Inc., 1973.

Da Costa, Phil. *100 Years of America's Fire Fighting Apparatus*. Los Angeles: Floyd Clymer Publications, 1964.

Dean, Anabel. *Fire! How Do They Fight It?* Philadelphia: The Westminster Press, 1978.

Hatmon, Paul W. *Yesterday's Fire Engines*. Minneapolis, Minnesota: Lerner Publications Company, 1980.

Holden, Raymond. *All About Fire*. New York: Random House, 1964.

Smith, Dennis, and Jill Freedman. *Firehouse*. Garden City, New York: Doubleday & Company, Inc., 1977.

Tamarin, Alfred. *Fire Fighting in America*. New York: The MacMillan Company, 1971.

CHICAGO AND WESTWARD EXPANSION

Havighurst, Walter, Ed. *Midwest and Great Plains*. Grand Rapids, Michigan: The Fideler Co., 1979.

Kogan, Herman, and Rick Kogan. *Yesterday's Chicago*. Miami, Florida: E.A. Seemann Publishing, Inc.

McCracken, Harold. *Winning of the West*. New York: Garden City Books, 1955.

Nash, Jay Robert. *People to See*. Piscataway, New Jersey: New Century Publishers, Inc., 1981.

Stein, R. Conrad. *America the Beautiful: Illinois*. Chicago: Children's Press, 1987.

Tunis, Edwin. *Frontier Living*. Cleveland, Ohio: World Publishing Company, 1961.

Wright, Louis B. *Everyday Life on the American Frontier*. New York: G.P. Putnam's Sons, 1968.

Other Works Consulted

Bare, William K. *Fundamentals of Fire Prevention*. New York: John Wiley & Sons, 1977.

Chlad, Dorothy. *When There Is a Fire...Go Outside*. Chicago: Childrens Press, 1982.

Colbert, Elias, and Everett Chamberlin. *Chicago and the Great Conflagration* (Facsimile ed.). New York: Viking Press, 1971. (Originally pub. 1871.)

Cromie, Robert. *The Great Chicago Fire*. New York: McGraw-Hill, 1958.

Evans, Hilary, and Mary Evans. *The Victorians: At Home and at Work*. New York: Arco Publishing Company, Inc., 1973.

Evans, R.J. *The Victorian Age 1815-1914*. New York: St. Martin's Press, 1968.

Gernsheim, Alison. *Victorian and Edwardian Fashion: A Photographic Survey*. New York: Dover Publications, Inc., 1981.

Heise, Kenan, and Mark Frazel. *Hands On Chicago*. Chicago: Bonus Books, 1987.

James, Derek. *Fire Prevention Handbook*. Cambridge, England: Butterworth & Company Ltd., 1986.

Mayer, Harold M., and Richard C. Wade. *Chicago: Growth of a Metropolis*. Chicago: The University of Chicago Press, 1969.

Pacyga, Dominic A., and Ellen Skerrett. *Chicago: City of Neighborhoods*. Chicago: Loyola University Press, 1986.

Waskin, Mel. *Mrs. O'Leary's Comet!* Chicago: Academy Chicago Publishers, 1985.

Index

The Author, Lois Warburton, earned her Masters degree in education at Clark University in Worcester, Massachusetts. Her previous published works include nonfiction articles, newspaper and magazine columns, and short stories. She is president of The Wordwright, a firm providing writing services to authors, businesses, and individuals. This is her first of three books for Lucent Books.

Illustrations designed by Maurie Manning capture the drama of the events described in this book.

Manning majored in illustration at Massachusetts College of Art in Boston and has been a professional children's illustrator for more than six years. Her work appears regularly in such magazines as *Children's Digest, Humpty Dumpty,* and *Highlights for Children.*

Manning was assisted by a team of three artists, Michael Spackman, Robert Caldwell, and Randol Eagles. A professional painter for more than nineteen years, Michael Spackman received his training at the High Museum Academy of Art in Atlanta. Robert Caldwell, a graduate of Syracuse University with a degree in fine arts, has been a fine arts professional for eight years. Randol Eagles is a specialist in figurative illustration, and has been a professional illustrator for three years.

Photography Credits

All photos courtesy of Chicago Historical Society
Clark Street at North Avenue, Chicago, Illinois, 60614